MW00623206

TALL ORDER!

Seven master strategies
to organize your life
and double your success
in half the time

Honorée Corpron

Published by Leading Edge Publishing, LLC

Printed in the United States of America.
ISBN 1-59872-390-1

Warning – Disclaimer
The purpose of this book is to educate and entertain. If you're not educated and entertained, it's your fault, not mine.

Contents

WHERE ARE YOU NOW?

Do you desire to make more money in less time? Create the business and career of your dreams? Enjoy a greater level of success while maintaining balance and fulfillment? If so, this book is for you!

There are many powerful strategies I have found myself consistently using and sharing with my coaching and corporate clients. This book includes seven of them.

If you want to take your life and business to the next level, you need clarity. Clarity includes an inspiring vision, precise goals, and a focused, exciting plan. You'll need to glean information from successful individuals who have gone before you. You need to have strategic success systems in place to allow you to be more effective and more efficient. You'll need to be cognizant of who and what you allow to surround you. Finally, you'll need to have someone who holds your vision for you and with you; cheers you on and gives you permission to go for it; and someone to hold you accountable when the going gets tough.

Tall Order! is the book to get you going in the right direction! Are you ready? Let's go! To your best success!

Honorée Corpron

Visionary, Strategist, Writer, Coach, Mom

"Some men see
things as they are
and say, "Why?" –
I dream of things
that never were and
say, "Why not?"

-- George Bernard Shaw

"I observe people
trying to be
successful and
my thought is,
"What the hell are
they thinking?"

-- Honorée Corpron

HOW ABOUT YOUR FAVORITE MARTINI?

When you go to a restaurant, you have the opportunity to "have it your way" – you can send your entrée back as many times as necessary until its done right. After all, you've gone to all the trouble of getting yourself there … of course you expect your order to be exactly the way you want it, right?

The same is true with your business – and your life. Here's some great news: Every moment of your life is a moment of creation. With this book, you are entering your next moments of creation with the assistance you need to help you to "order" – if you will – your destiny just exactly the way you want it.

I am presenting to you a collection of strategies, formulas, tips, tools, and ideas that I use, and I know they work because they work for me and my clients – every single day.

Here's what I suggest you do: take each element, decide if it resonates for you. If it does, take what of it works and put it into operation. Tweak and refine as necessary until you've "cracked your code." Soon you'll be experiencing a greater level of success and fulfillment than you thought possible.

"We go where our vision is."

-- Joseph Murphy

"Travel in the direction of your clear vision ... and take your road map just in case."

-- Honorée Corpron

MASTER STRATEGY #1: ENVISIONING YOUR VISION

At my daughter's karate school, her instructor repeats over and over: "Focus on the target!" Whatever stage of business you find yourself in, if you haven't defined a clear precise vision up to this point, ***now is the time to create one***.

Vision is what you see in your mind's eye, not something you see externally. Do you go on a trip without knowing your destination? Of course not. The first master strategy is *creating your vision*. Personally, this is my favorite strategy. You will find it to be a most exciting strategy and big fun to put together.

At first, the process and outcomes of visioning may seem vague and intangible. But the long-term benefits are beneficial, substantial, and the results can be simply amazing.

Visioning breaks you out of boundary thinking. As you open your mind and your mind's eye to new possibilities, you will begin to shed previous limitations.

Visioning provides continuity and avoids the stutter effect of planning fits and starts. Having a defined, clear vision that is reviewed often – I recommend daily – will help you avoid "New Year's Eve Syndrome" … where goals are set, then forgotten in about two weeks (until the next New Year)!

Your vision automatically identifies your future direction and purpose. It grabs hold of your interest, strengthens your commitment and promotes laser-like focus. When there is a clear picture in your mind of where you're going, it is always there, accessible -- readily available to pull you in the right direction.

Visioning encourages openness to unique and creative solutions. As you hold your clearly defined vision, the ways to make that vision happen become clear. Your subconscious mind works on your behalf to spot potential opportunities, prospects, and possibilities you might otherwise have missed.

Visioning promotes and builds confidence. Have you ever noticed how a person who has a purpose and a vision carries themselves in a certain way? They are positive, upbeat, and yes, confident. Your confidence is magnetic, attracting to you your clearly defined vision.

COACH'S INSIGHT: *You have already created in your life what you have previously held as a vision – even if you didn't realize that's what you were doing. Now is the time to use your subconscious mind through the use of this picturing tool to create what you truly desire, this time on purpose.*

Think of vision as clear imagination – only now directed imagination … creating your future, one magical moment at a time.

YOUR VISIONING EXERCISE

Start by daydreaming. Begin to imagine what your business and life would look like if time, energy, people, space and money were no object. What areas of your business need a clearer vision? How can your marketing, advertising, or customer service divisions be markedly improved? What areas of your life aren't working as well as you would like? Are you in an empowering relationship that is mutually-beneficial? Are you as strong, fit, financially sound, balanced and fulfilled as you wish to be?

Create an overall vision, then break your vision down into focus areas and create a unique vision for each of those areas. Begin by starting five to ten years in the future. Describe in vivid detail what your ideal day looks like. Include a description of your surroundings (office, employees, clients, family and friends). Now work backward from that vision. Describe what that vision looks like in six months, then three, and finally next week. Ask yourself, "What is my preferred future?" being sure to:

Draw on your beliefs, mission, and mental picture of your model environment.

Describe in detail what you want to see in the future.

Be specific to each area of your life.

Be positive and inspired.

Be open to massive changes!

Here are some questions to get you started creating your vision:

- In your vision, what time does your day start? End?
- Who is with you? Your success is determined in large part by the people you surround yourself with, and it's time to become clear about who you want to attract into your life in the future. We'll address this more in Chapter 6.
- What activities are included in your ideal day (exercise, meetings, phone calls, fun, meditation)?
- What types of customers do you have? Create an ideal client list with at least 25 characteristics of the model client. Include everything from age, income, and attitude, to how they receive information and services from you and how often they refer new business to you.
- Where is your office located? Do you have multiple locations? Do you work from home or in the office, or from both places? Be sure to include the type of equipment you work with, all those neat furnishings, plants, pictures, etc.
- Do you have employees? How many?
- What is your ideal living space? Where is it located? What do you drive?
- Where do you vacation? With who? How often?
- Define your friends and other significant relationships.

Brainstorm. Be specific. Be playful. Be creative. Make it the way you want it … after all, *it's your life!*

> **COACH'S NOTE:** *It is important to put your vision in writing. There is power in the written word. Just the act of writing down what you want sets the creative process in motion.*

VISION KILLERS

As you engage in the visioning process, be alert to the following vision killers:

> **Tradition. Be careful of the phrase: "But we've always done it this way."**
>
> **Fear of ridicule. Most often the people who criticize are those who have neglected to create their own vision, who come from a place of fear instead of power.**
>
> **Stereotypes of people, conditions, roles and outcomes.**
>
> **Nay-sayers. Very simply, refuse to listen to anyone who doesn't absolutely 100% support your vision. Period.**

Remember: there is no right or wrong way to write a vision! You should describe in full detail exactly what you desire. It may take up to 20 pages or more, or it may be as simple as one page using bullet points.

> **COACH'S CHALLENGE:** *Stop here and create your vision. Before you can create any goal, a clear picture of your overall vision must be present in your mind's eye. Do it now – or schedule a non-negotiable appointment with yourself to do this first, most important step.*

"Your legacy is the powerful, positive impact you have on others."

-- Honorée Corpron

A great example of someone who has created a compelling vision is Margaret Trost, Founder and President of the *What If? Foundation*. After a visit to Haiti in 2000, Margaret created a vision for feeding the hungry children she met in an impoverished neighborhood in Port-au-Prince. It started out as a dream to feed the children, then grew into a vision to provide 350 meals per week, even though she wasn't sure exactly how to do it. Over time her vision continued to expand. Today Margaret's foundation provides over 1500 meals a week and sends several children to school. "My vision keeps expanding, always inspiring me to do what I can to make it happen."

Margaret believes and knows from experience that a vision must come from within – a product of the heart. When it's right, the general feeling will be, "Oh my goodness! … I'm so excited and inspired! I have chills … I'm not exactly sure how I'm going to do this, but I sure am determined to do everything I can to make it happen!"

She also shared that the true power of vision comes into play as the daily challenges of life surface, as set-backs appear. A true, from-the-heart vision will keep you focused, moving forward, even when it might be easier to quit or give up. She lives by the wonderful Creole saying, "Piti piti n a rivé" -- "Little by little, we will arrive."

To learn more about the What If? Foundation, go to www.whatiffoundation.org.

"You are not here merely to make a living. You are here to enable the world to live more amply, with greater vision, and with a finer spirit of hope and achievement. You are here to enrich the world. You impoverish yourself if you forget this errand."

-- Woodrow Wilson
(1856-1924)

"All successful people have a goal. No one can get anywhere unless he knows where he wants to go and what he wants to be or do."

-- Norman Vincent Peale

"If you are not able to see your goals, they will take longer to achieve, and sometimes "longer" is "never."

-- Honorée Corpron

MASTER STRATEGY #2: VISIBLE GOALS

Now that your vision is in your mind's eye, what may be going through your mind right now is a combination of "Wow, let's go!" and "Uh-oh, what do I do next?"

The great news is that by having a clear, compelling vision, you have a wonderful place to start. Are you fired up? A great vision inspires, motivates and drives you forward. It will also pull you forward effortlessly.

You should feel excited, perhaps a little apprehensive. This is normal, just go with it. Your goals should be big enough to make you feel "stretched," — you can do it with some effort; and yet not so big that your mind checks out.

Based on the areas you focused on in your vision, the next step is to identify categories within those areas such as: employees, money, exercise, family and personal time, personal development and other "things" you want to acquire. How much new business will you produce? How many new customers? How many new employees? How much money are you generating? Where are you going on vacation? What new car do you want to drive?

With each successive piece, you'll achieve greater clarity (sounding familiar?).

Suppose you want to make $30,000 this month, and each sale of your product or service is $2,500. Do the math. You'll need twelve customers to reach your goal. Be as specific as possible. Words like *more*, *a lot*, *some* are too vague. There is power in precision.

COACH'S COMMANDMENTS FOR GOAL-SETTING:

❶ Write down your goals. This is the most important aspect of goal-setting: Writing down your goals creates the roadmap to your success.

> **COACH'S INSIGHT:** *Although just the act of writing them down can set the process in motion, it's also extremely important to review your goals frequently. Remember, the more focused you are on your goals the more likely you are to accomplish them.*

Sometimes we realize we have to revise a goal as circumstances and other goals change. If you need to change a goal, don't consider it a failure. Instead, consider it a victory because you had the insight to realize the goal you set wasn't perfect and you had the courage to make a change!

"Write it down.
Written goals have a
way of transforming
wishes into wants;
cant's into cans;
dreams into plans;
and plans into reality.
Don't just think it --
ink it!"

-- Author Unknown

"If you don't see it,
you will be never
be it."

-- Author Known (me)

❷ Your goals should be based solely on your vision.

Write your goals in positive language. Define and work for what you want, not what you want to leave behind. You are using language to focus your brain in the exact direction your want it to take you. Part of the reason for writing down, examining and re-examining your goals is to create a set of instructions for your subconscious mind to carry out. *Your subconscious mind is a very efficient, powerful tool that does not distinguish the real from the imagined, and it does not judge.* Its only function is to carry out instructions. The more positive instructions you give it, the more positive results you will get, and the faster you will get them.

> **COACH'S COMMAND:** *Positive thinking should not be limited to goal-setting, either. Apply it in everyday life to help you grow as a human being, too.*

❸ Make your goals congruent with each other.

In other words, one goal must not contradict any of your other goals.

> **COACH'S EXAMPLE:** *A goal to buy a $750,000 home is incongruent with an income goal of $50,000 per year. This is called non-integrated thinking and will sabotage all of the hard work you put into your goals. Non-integrated thinking can also hamper your everyday thoughts as well.*

❹ Make your goals specific, precise, clearly defined.

Just like your vision, write out your goals in complete, vivid detail! Instead of writing "a new home," describe the home you desire: "A 7,500 square foot contemporary with 5 bedrooms, 3 baths, an office with a separate entrance, and a view of the mountains on 20 acres of land."

Once again, giving the subconscious mind a detailed set of instructions is crucial to goal achievement. The more clear, specific information you give the subconscious mind, the clearer the final outcome becomes, and the more efficiently the subconscious works to turn your dreams into reality.

Can you close your eyes and visualize the home I described above? Walk around the house. Stand on the porch off the master bedroom and see the fog lifting off the mountains. Look down at the garden full of tomatoes, green beans and cucumbers. Off to the right is the other garden full of mums, carnations and roses. Can you see it? So can your subconscious mind, and it will work relentlessly to bring your vision to reality as quickly as possible, in the exact way you have imagined.

> **COACH'S NOTE:** *This is where your mind has worked "for you" yet seemingly against you in the past. It has created what you have previously held in your mind as your vision. This is another reason to have a clearly-defined, written vision.*

❺ Include a timeline.

Timelines are vital to goal achievement. By when, **exactly**, must this goal be achieved? "This year," "soon," "in a little while," or "later" doesn't cut it. Pick a date. If it's not on the calendar, it's not going to happen. Your timeline will need to be written like: "By June 30th, I have 12 new customers who purchase my services at $2,500 each." You must be able to measure exactly where you stand now against where you want to be in the future.

"A goal is a dream with a deadline."

--Napoleon Hill

❻ Make sure your goals are big enough!

I'm sure you've heard the old saying, "Shoot for the moon. If you miss you'll still reach the stars." Goals should inspire you to move forward, perhaps with a little bit of a knot in your stomach. If your goals are too easy, you won't be as motivated to achieve them. If they're too hard, you might become overwhelmed and not even take the first, necessary steps.

> **COACH'S CHALLENGE:** *Set your goals now. (Is there going to be a better time?) Taking action right away reinforces to your subconscious mind you are serious about achieving your vision.*

WHAT'S NEXT?

I recommend that you keep your goals to yourself. Share them only with those people you absolutely, 100% know will support and encourage you. Stay away from "dream stealers." Negative attitudes from friends and family can drag you down at the speed of sound. It's critical that your self-talk (the thoughts in your head), and the talk around you are positive.

Reviewing your goals daily is crucial to your success and must become part of your routine.

> **COACH'S SUGGESTION:** *Make copies to put in different places in your office, car and home to keep you on track. I post my goals everywhere – above my treadmill, on my bathroom mirror, on my desk, in my car. I want to be reminded of what I want to have, do, be and create in every possible moment.*

Each morning when you wake up, read your list of goals. Spend a few moments visualizing each goal as completed: see your new completely furnished home, smell the leather seats in your hot new sports car, *feel* the cold hard cash in your hands (or, in my case, using my MasterCard at Nordstrom's … often). Visualize yourself on that vacation to sunny Mexico, the sun warm on your skin as you sip piña coladas beside the clear blue ocean. Vividly picturing your goals completed triggers your brain to automatically move you toward your vision as quickly as possible.

Each night just before bed, repeat the process. This will start both your conscious and subconscious mind working towards your goals. Replace any negative self-talk and images with the positive energy you need to move forward.

Every time you make a decision or take an action during the day, ask yourself: "Does this take me closer to or further away from, my goal?" If the answer is "closer to," then you've made the right decision. If the answer is "further from," well … you know what to do!

Follow this process everyday, and you'll be on your way to achieving unlimited success in every aspect of your life.

Keahi Pelayo, a realtor in Honolulu, inspired me recently when I asked him to share with me his distinctions (those things that are distinguished as a higher level of excellence through observation) about goal setting. As a highly successful person, he had achieved all of his "thing" goals … the house, the cars, the vacations, the trinkets.

What then, I wondered, does one use to keep themselves motivated to continue to move forward, when seemingly "enough is enough?" The answer, my friends, is leverage. Leverage is the act of using external factors to keep you on track; it improves and enhances your power to act effectively.

Keahi shared with me a recent powerful goal-setting experience. The market in Honolulu was going exceptionally well, and he had set the goal of doing more business in that month than ever before. I was intrigued. His goal was to do seven listings and eight sales in that month. Further, he was using the power of leverage to reach his goal. I was more intrigued.

His son, age six, had told his dad he really wanted to have a new train. Keahi told his son about his big goals and made a deal with him: if Keahi achieved his goals, his son would get his train. If he didn't, there would be no train. His son was to check with him often (and, as any parent knows, in child-speak, that is about every 10 minutes) to see how dad was coming on the goals, if he had achieved them, and when the train would be forthcoming.

Needless to say, his son was relentless (leverage can be very powerful!). The goals were achieved, his son got his train, and everyone was happy.

> **COACH'S PRACTICE-IN-ACTION:** *Using affirmations will rapidly increase your results! I also call affirmations "vision-to-reality" statements. Your goals, stated in the form of present tense, positive statements produce fast, often amazing results. Be sure to include words that excite and motivate you in your affirmations!*

Affirmations are vital ingredients in the recipe for success and personal well being. After all, whether you think you can or you can't, you're right. Many of the world's most successful people have testified to the power of affirmations. Affirmations reflect what you *believe* to be true.

Here are some examples of affirmations:

- **I can't do it.**
- **I hate myself.**
- **I'm ugly.**
- **I'm stupid.**
- **I knew I would mess up.**

Surprised you, didn't I? You thought affirmations were only positive things you say to yourself. Affirmations are simply thoughts you repeat or "affirm" so often you believe they're true. They can be positive or negative. They solidify any thought or idea you have. They can work to your advantage or disadvantage. They will be your strongest supporters or your greatest obstacles. The beauty of affirmations is that you control them once you're aware that you're already using them.

> **COACH'S HINT:** *You can change what you believe to be true by using affirmations. You are already using them. Now is the time to create new ones that move you in the direction of your vision and goals.*

Start listening to your internal dialog. You may be surprised to find just how often you say negative things to yourself … about you. Use your journal to record your negative self-talk for one day. The results will shock you (and not in a good way!). You will be surprised how many negative thoughts you are having, and how often you say something negative to yourself about you!

Once you have identified the negative affirmations, you can replace them with positive, confident and empowering thoughts. Remember nothing we experience comes labeled; we label it. The power to choose is yours.

Look at the difference:

- **I can do it!**
- **I love myself!**
- **I am beautiful!**
- **I am smart!**
- **I am successful!**
- **I know I can do it!**

If you plant rose seeds you get roses. Plant seeds of happiness, success, hope and love; they will come back to you in abundance. This is the law of nature. Choose to surround yourself with positive influences. Affirm positive statements daily until they become second nature. You'll soon begin to harvest a crop of positive results in your life. "Negatives" belong in a photographer's studio, not in your mind.

EXAMPLE:

GOAL: To increase my business by 50 monthly consumers by March 31, 2006.

AFFIRMATION: "I am jazzed as my business now increases by 50 consumers each month."

MY PERSONAL FAVORITE AFFIRMATION: "I am an irresistible magnet for unlimited money, clients, goods and services every single day!"

Do your affirmations out loud, with passion, while exercising, while you're in the shower, driving, or waiting in line at the bank (these could be silent). You'll be amazed by the results! For my top 10 favorite affirmations, log onto my Web site at www.Corpron.com to download your free copy!

"Action is the foundational key to all success."

-- Anthony Robbins

"Action without an action plan is wasted action."

-- Honorée Corpron

MASTER STRATEGY #3: 100-DAY ACTION PLAN

What I'm doing right now in my business will show up as results in three months. Why? Because of "lag time." True momentum is gained over time. I have discovered it takes about 100 days for the results of my actions to really become evident. I call this the 100-Day Rule, and you'll need to create a 100-Day Plan to keep you focused and moving in the right direction.

I was recently at a seminar where the 100-Day Rule was discussed. It got me reflecting on my network marketing days and how much of an impact this rule made on my business. I also realized the impact it has on my current businesses!

Here's how the 100-Day Rule works. Whatever you are doing right now, today, will affect your business in 100 days. If you're busy searching for new business two hours a day, you'll have fantastic results in 100 days. If you occupy yourself with paperwork and minutiae, allowing them to consume all of your time, then 100 days from now you're going to be frustrated because you won't be generating the results I know you truly desire.

After a short time working together, clients will often ask me, "What is the problem – why aren't things happening for me now?" My response is (always): "What were you doing 100 days ago?" Those are the results you're getting today! It should make you think, and open your eyes to realize the importance of today's activities, and the thoughts, you are (or are not) putting into pre-planning them.

I often see my clients get focused, take massive action, network, make phone calls, have a calendar full of meetings, and see no immediate results in month one. They see some measurable results in month two, and then, bang! Amazing results and true momentum occur for them in month three.

The 100-day Rule will keep you going because it will help you understand what is happening in your business and why. You're less likely to become discouraged and quit when you understand this concept. It's fun to be looking days ahead, and it takes the pressure off while you're working your current plan.

Don't beat yourself up for what you did, or didn't do, 100 days ago. It's what you do today that is important. When you accept this rule, it's much easier to persevere in the face of "downturns."

"We have time enough if we will but use it aright."

— Johann Wolfgang von Goethe

"Determine how you will use your time well in advance … and the results will speak for themselves."

— Honorée Corpron

> **COACH'S COMMAND:** *To create a strong, stable, constantly growing business, always be thinking and working 100 days out.*

Here's how to make sure your business plan pays off: create a 100-Day Plan, and update it every single month. Meaning, you will actually create 12 100-Day Plans each year … starting with January 1st – March 10th, then the beginning of February, create a new 100-Day Plan – the dates of this one will be February 1st – April 10th. This will keep you consistently moving in the right direction, with on-going, effective check-ins to keep you on track.

Begin your 100-Day Plan with a mini-vision statement, accompanied by a purpose statement. These two statements will be your guiding light, reminding you not only what you're excited about, but why.

Next, create empowering descriptors for yourself, such as "progressive, educated leader" or "marketing maven." In other words, do you want to be "in shape" or a "goddess?" Give yourself a reputation to live up to, using the most energizing, positive words you can think of. Words are incredibly powerful, be particularly alert to the words you use to describe yourself and the actions you want to take. These powerful descriptions of you will help create and maintain a desire to continue, even when the going gets tough.

Your plan should include three areas of focus. Depending on which areas of your business need growth, development and management, you'll pick the three most important.

> **COACH'S INSIGHT:** *The brain can only handle three ideas at one time. Have you heard of 1-2-3-many? This phrase refers to how much the brain can handle when given information. When providing directions to your home, most people can remember "take a left at the Texaco, then a right on Elm, it's the third house on the right." Those three pieces of information can be recalled easily. More than that is too many.*

The same "principle of three" applies to your business. Do you need more contacts? Are you getting, but not closing, presentations? Do you have plenty of customers, but want to improve your relationship with them? Pick the top three, most crucial to be the focus areas for this particular 100-Day Plan. Keep in mind that you'll be re-tooling, modifying and updating your plan monthly. You want your plan, and your business, to be balanced.

> **COACH'S EXAMPLE:** *As you are focusing on current sales, remember to look for new business and be constantly networking to keep your momentum going.*

Next, define your resources. I'm not talking about cash resources here. I'm talking about people you know, books, seminars, and other business tools. Your resources are invaluable, in that they are a well you can draw from to maximize results. The more resources you have available, the easier your path to success can be.

Of course, you'll add in your goals – making them to fit within the 100-Day timeframe.

The last section of your 100-day Plan is the "Next Steps" section. This includes everything you can think of that needs to be done for you to reach your goals in the next 100 days. Like a to-do list, you are going to prioritize each item according to what is most important, then what's next most important … repeating until the list is completed.

Below is an actual example that you can use as a model for your own.

100-DAY PLAN EXAMPLE, created by Zac Sestina, a successful realtor with Keller-Williams in San Diego:

100-DAY VISION: Create an ever-increasing income of more than $25,000 monthly. Connect homes to new homeowners.

100-DAY PURPOSE: Increase to 10 monthly transactions.

EMPOWERING DESCRIPTORS:

- **Progressive, learning-based leader**
- **Focused and productive**
- **Leads by example**
- **Results- and growth-driven**

100-DAY INTENTION: Increase monthly income to more than $25,000, and monthly transactions to more than 10, and make this automatic going forward.

THREE AREAS OF FOCUS:

1. Determine marketing methods in order to activate law of attraction
2. Create strategic partnerships and alliances.
3. Recruit listing agents for continued business expansion

RESOURCES:

1. Mentor 2. Networking 3. My coach

GOALS:

1. Five Listings/month by end of March
2. Five Sales/month by end of March
3. Hire a listing agent by end of January

NEXT STEPS:

1. Implement marketing based, prospecting enhanced lead generation system to targeted market.
2. Interview 10 Buyers Agents to hire (must have experience working with builders to add value to existing relationships).
3. Spend one half of current lead generation time interviewing potential staff members.
4. Create and maintain a one-year business and marketing budget. Hold it accountable to tangible results!
5. Spend three hours per workday soliciting referrals for new business and new staff members. Remember the Thank-You notes!

For a blank 100-Day Plan, log onto my Web site at www.Corpron.com to download your free copy!

THINGS TO REMEMBER:

- **It doesn't have to be perfect - just do it! You'll be changing, updating and refining often.**
- **Notice the results you're getting. Make adjustments and changes as necessary.**
- **Get excited - you're well on your way to creating exactly what you want!**

"Mentor: someone whose foresight can become your hindsight."

-- Unknown

"If you can find out what the most successful people did in any area and then you did the same thing over and over, you'd eventually get the same results they do."

-- Brian Tracy

"Crack your success code by duplicating, shifting and mastering the strategies of successful people."

-- Honorée Corpron

MASTER STRATEGY #4: FINDING A PERFECT MENTOR

Why reinvent the wheel? A mentor can help you turn decades into days (ok, maybe weeks) by giving you key information to make your journey easier, saving you time, energy, and money.

When you think of a mentor, you may visualize an experienced businessperson who would take you under their wing and teach you all about business, customers and relationships -- the one you wouldn't think about making a major decision without consulting. You want someone who has started a business in your industry, been successful and who has probably made many of the mistakes you hope to avoid.

The first challenge is deciding who would make the best mentor for you.

> **COACH'S QUESTION:** *"Who has already created the business or career that I want?" The successful person who has spent 10 years or more in your chosen field is the perfect person to model your business after.*

Before you pick up the phone, remember: preparation is key. You don't want to waste your time, or that of your potential mentor. Start by creating a list of questions you want to ask your potential mentor.

> **COACHING-IN-ACTION:** *Make a short list of potential mentor-candidates. Invite each of them to lunch or coffee, give them high praise for their accomplishments, and ask them to be your mentor.*

Perhaps your mentor will agree to be available to you on an ongoing basis, but for starters, a list of questions designed to get them talking about key distinctions you wish to make is important. That way, if it is a one-time meeting, you'll be able gather some important and potentially life-changing information in a short time frame.

SAMPLE QUESTIONS FOR YOUR MENTOR:

- If you had to do it all over again, what would you do differently?
- Where do you feel the industry is going?
- What, in your mind, is the difference between someone who is hugely successful, moderately successful and not at all successful in our business?
- What did you (and do you) have to believe about yourself to create the results you've created?

When I was ready to accelerate the growth of my network marketing business, I thought about who had the level of success, income, and lifestyle I aspired to create. A woman I had met on one occasion (and whose tapes and other materials I had used over and over) came to mind. Because she wasn't in my "upline" (and therefore did not benefit from helping me), I approached her through a third party. Turns out, this was unnecessary.

> **COACH'S NOTE:** *Most people are happy to give you an hour or two of their time, particularly if they know you are going to take action on the knowledge, insights and wisdom they share with you. The most successful people also tend to be the most gracious and willing to help.*

My mentor, Mollie Pratt, jumped at the chance to help me. She later told me that the reason she was so willing to help was because she saw my approaching her as a sign of my commitment and enthusiasm … and actually, feeling my energy and excitement helped to keep her motivated and moving forward in her business!

Few people will resist this approach: "I've admired what you've accomplished in this field. Would you allow me to take you to lunch and ask you a few questions?" When you do get that meeting, remember the more specific your questions, the more value you'll receive.

A mentor relationship can also develop into something deep, personal, and long term. A mentor is someone who serves as an example, an advisor, a sounding board, and in most cases ultimately a friend.

That last attribute is very important. A mentor cannot really be effective if they don't truly care for you, and vice versa. Great mentors do what they do for one reason: they want to help you succeed. They aren't working with you to make money, to boost their egos, or to be able to claim volunteer time on their resume. They work with you because they're interested in helping people.

Back to Mollie … through e-mail correspondence we agreed on a time for me to call her. I had compiled a list of twelve questions that I felt, if she answered, would help me to correctly set my future course and direction. I was honored and thrilled when Mollie agreed to chat with me and our initial conversations proved to be beneficial. She then agreed to work with me a few more times.

While this won't always be the case, know that your attitude, passion and dedication will bear heavily on someone else's willingness to help you!

Also, remember that you can have more than one mentor. Talking to folks of different ages, levels of experience and backgrounds can give you a well-rounded view of your industry, its trends and future.

> *"Reinvent the wheel? No way! The road to success has been paved by your mentors … combine their strategies with your enthusiasm and focus and your success is guaranteed!"*
>
> -- Honorée Corpron

COACH'S CLARIFICATION: Here are some things to think about as you seek your perfect mentor.

> **Earn their respect.**
>
> **Ask nicely.**
>
> **Be prepared.**
>
> **Always be on time (if you're less than 10 minutes early, you're late!).**
>
> **Find common ground. Did you attend the same college or university? Are you from the same state or town? Perhaps you have something besides your industry in common, such as a hobby or religion.**
>
> **Always, always, always be respectful of your mentor's time.**
>
> **Be sure to acknowledge them with a handwritten thank-you note after each meeting and phone conversation.**
>
> **Be aware of how generous they are, because hopefully, someday, you will be a mentor!**

"Be steady and well ordered in your life so that you can be fierce and original in your work."

-- Gustave Flaubert

"In order for any system or strategy to work, its up to you to take the first step. The structure will set you free!"

-- Honorée Corpron

MASTER STRATEGY #5: STRATEGIC SUCCESS SYSTEMS

A major part of the work I do with my coaching clients centers around the systems they have in place, don't have in place, and need and want to put in place. These systems help to increase their levels of efficiency and effectiveness when it comes to the best use of their time, employee recruiting and retention, business expansion and crisis management.

More than half of my clients have come to me because they're working more hours than they want to, they aren't spending time with their families, and their hobbies are severely neglected or long since forgotten. (The other half wants to make more money in less time. Imagine that!)

Here are two of the most aggressive strategies you can apply today to dramatically increase your effectiveness and efficiency immediately.

These are what I call "Multiplier Strategies." That means they will multiply and improve your current level of efficiency dramatically. A word of warning: these strategies are powerful … be prepared!

By now you've taken care of the basics of optimizing your time, such as obtaining a PDA, and hiring an assistant to handle your day-to-day activities. You'll get good results with the fundamentals, and there's another level for you when you optimize your normal workday.

With that said, here we go!

MULTIPLIER TIME-LEVERAGING STRATEGY NUMBER ONE: One morning hour (your "Power Hour") equals two evening hours. Get up and into the office one or even two hours earlier than you have up until now. You will find you will be able to accomplish twice as much in any given early morning hour, as you will in one evening hour.

Chances are you'll be less mentally alert in the evening, especially if you have worked a full day. If your most productive hours are late at night or you're simply not a morning person, you can use late night hours as your "power hour" time. The key is to determine what time of day your mind if most clear, focused and energized, and to dedicate that time to working on your business. In coaching, I call this "your edge."

This strategy is why the world's top business owners can be found in their offices hours much earlier than those less successful. To join the ranks of other outrageously successful business people, you will want to be found in your office right along with them. If you've picked up this book, it's probably because you're not part of "the pack," or at the very least you're tired of being there!

You will use your power hour to handle the most important aspects of your day: strategic planning, scheduling, and systems. By doing this before anyone else even begins working, you've gained control of the flow of the rest of your day.

If you don't (or you haven't), you'll find yourself reacting to the events of the day instead of being able to respond to them. This makes you "response-able." Your power hour is when you should be focused only on actions that take you closer to your long-range goals.

This is not the time to catch up on e-mail, handle short-term actions or work on paperwork. Those tasks are all time traps, and if you succumb to them, you'll never gain the exponential multiplication of quality, focused time you're after! You'll put those into your schedule, purpose in a time slot where you don't need to be on your "A" game. Delegating these simple tasks to your assistant will also multiply your efficiency and effectiveness.

Here's a simple example: imagine a five-year-old boy with a small chunk of Kryptonite sneaking up on Superman while he sleeps. If Superman doesn't see him coming, he's trapped. It doesn't matter that Superman is a superior adversary. A little boy has gained control of Superman's time; consequently he is now in control of Superman.

It's the same thing with your average workday. If you start your workday when everyone else does, you'll be trying to perform and produce in the most difficult of circumstances.

Even the most efficient businessperson will lose the upper hand to the "busy-ness" of the average workday. If you try to optimize the hours between 8 a.m. and 5 p.m. beyond a certain point, you are fighting your daily battle to succeed while dealing with interruptions, urgencies and employee challenges. You already know how these can wreak havoc on your time.

Once you use your early morning power hour for long-term goal activities, your enemy (busy-ness) can never take them away.

MULTIPLIER TIME-LEVERAGING STRATEGY NUMBER TWO: One weekly planning hour equals 200%+ increased ability and success.

I advise my clients to spend at least one hour on Friday afternoon or over the weekend to create their Weekly Plan. This strategy allows you to block time for the people, things and events most important to you – ahead of time.

Perhaps you've seen the time management demonstration including large rocks, small pebbles, sand, and water – all meant to be put into a jar. Each element represents items on your to do list, in order of importance. When you put the water in first, try putting in sand and see what happens. The water comes out. Fill it up with sand, the pebbles and rocks don't stand a chance.

The most effective way to put all four elements in is in this order: rocks (the most important things in your life and business), pebbles (the next most important items), sand (items with no urgency at all), and water (least important stuff to do, delegate or discard). Amazingly, these four elements will all fit into your "time jar" –when you start with the largest (most important) items first. If some of the smaller elements don't fit or go by the wayside, it just doesn't matter as much.

How does this translate to your life and business? Schedule in advance the most important things you want to accomplish, as they relate to your long-term goals. Block the time out and don't let anything change your focus.

Anything, you say? Yes, anything!

I call it "brain surgery time." Here's the analogy: five minutes from now you fall to the floor, unconscious. After being rushed to the emergency room, doctors run tests and determine you need brain surgery.

Good news! The most respected and highly skilled brain surgeon in the world is available to work on you (and miraculously, he's covered by your insurance). He's available tomorrow from 10 a.m. until 3 p.m. to complete the five hours of surgery necessary to save your life. Can you think of any reason you would miss the opportunity to have him do your surgery? Of course not!

When you schedule time to do what needs to be done, time working on your business, quality time with your family, your kids, and yourself, you must treat it like "brain surgery time." Of course you can be flexible – and you can also learn to stay focused on what is truly important.

> *"We all have the same*
> *24-hours each day.*
> *The difference*
> *between your future*
> *success or failure is up*
> *to you, your attitude*
> *and where you focus*
> *your time."*
>
> -- Honorée Corpron

Schedule an hour each week to do your planning. Turn off the phones, pagers, cell phones, email and television. Block out time for what's most important.

Ask yourself:

> **Who needs to hear from you (customers, vendors, potential business, prospects, business partners, investors)? Remember your 100-Day Plan.**
>
> **Who needs to see you (family, friends, and perhaps you need a little time with yourself)?**
>
> **What needs to be done, organized, planned, and executed?**

Using these two time-multiplier strategies will produce a huge difference right away. Your productivity will skyrocket to more than double what it's been in the past. You'll also be energized by all you've accomplished, including the non-business related items.

"Pay any price to stay in the presence of extraordinary people."

-- Mike Murdock

"The only difference between where you are this year and where you are next, are the books you read, the people you meet, and the actions you take."

-- Charlie "Tremendous" Jones

"You will eventually rise to the level of the people you hang around with – whether you hang around millionaires or idiots."

-- Honorée Corpron

MASTER STRATEGY #6: THE POWER OF ASSOCIATION

Who and what you have in your life determines whether or not you succeed. Harsh? Perhaps. True? Absolutely. You see, your environment – which is comprised of your home, where you work, your friends and associates – determines with great accuracy whether you will be successful ... *or not*.

When I was full-force building my network marketing business, I easily found lots of people who wanted my lifestyle. What they didn't always want was to do the work it took to achieve it! For less than $200 you can start a business that with hard work, focus and determination can yield incomes in the six- and seven-figure levels. Of course I heard a lot of "sign me up for that!"

I found it frustrating, however, to want to coach, mentor and develop my business partners to a respectable income level, only to have some of them quit after a short time (and usually inches before they were about to see the big results they desired).

At the peak of my displeasure, I received a destiny-changing phone call from a respected business colleague. He asked me a particularly powerful question, one of the best I have ever heard: "Do you realize that success in business (or life) is determined not in who you hire, but in who you fail to fire?"

That question prompted me to revisit my vision of the ultimate business partner – who I *really* wanted to work with, what I would expect of them and of myself in our on-going relationship.

Then, about five years ago I was contemplating a huge career change in my life. Having just accomplished my long-term business goals, I was quickly losing interest in my career. I'll be honest – life was great! I had recently attended my company's international convention and received multiple awards. My income was substantial and sustaining. Yet, internally I was unsettled and knew it was time to move to another level.

Another powerful phone call changed my trajectory. A long-time friend asked me the mother of all power questions: "Who do you have in your life asking you a better question every single day, challenging you to be the best you can be?" She knew it would be easy for me to stay in my comfort zone, to ignore my restlessness and become complacent.

In truth, while I had lots of loving and wonderful people around me, the number of people challenging me to be my best on a daily basis was almost non-existent. I realized that in order to take my life to the next level, I needed a level of support that did not exist for me. I needed to find more people living the life I aspired to live, who would be willing to push me, pull me, entice me and encourage me each and every day. With her encouragement, that of my coach and a few close friends, I made the decision to change careers.

Once I stepped through the fear and made the decision to make the career transition, everything fell into place.

These two questions, at exactly the right times in my life, gave me ultimate clarity. They pointed out to me that the choices I was making in my relationships and business were holding me back, and not allowing me to move forward.

How does this relate to you? Perhaps the people around you don't bring out the best in you. They don't challenge you to expect results you think may be impossible. Maybe your career isn't the best fit. Are you living in an environment that you don't absolutely love?

COACH'S OBSERVATION: Here's what happens when you take control of your environment, including everyone and everything in it:

> **You'll suddenly have tons of more energy! Things will happen faster, easier, and better than ever before.**
>
> **You will be much more creative! You'll create synergy with the old and new people in your life, which will automatically take you higher.**
>
> **You'll have much less stress! As you streamline the details of your life, you get rid of the old baggage and create more room for new and exciting opportunities.**

In coaching, we talk a lot about "tolerations." Tolerations are those things that zap your energy, annoy you, and drain away your effectiveness, happiness and success. They make you less attractive to yourself, and therefore, less attractive to others. You have three choices with tolerations: change them, eliminate them, or accept them.

Your environment, including the people in it, is crucial to your success or failure. Think about each person in your life: are they supportive of your vision? Your goals? Do they ask you empowering, and if necessary, tough questions? Or do they predict failure, doom or worse? Be aware of what your friends, family, and associates bring to your life. If they are not empowering you to be your best, perhaps its time for them to go! You won't need to necessarily usher people out of your life, just keep your distance. Look at it this way: there are many people you want to stay in touch with, people you admire ... Those relationships that are no longer in your best interest can be allowed to fade away. It's that easy.

Is your home your sanctuary? Do you feel comfortable, relaxed, creative and alive there? If not, make it the way you want it to be. Again, it is your life!

By taking control of your immediate environment, you reclaim your personal power and set a healthy focused foundation for your future.

"Surround yourself with people who are going to lift you higher."

-- Oprah Winfrey

"A Coach is someone who tells you what you don't want to hear, who has you see what you don't want to see, so you can be who you have always known you could be."

-- Tom Landry

"Ability is what you're capable of doing. Motivation determines what you do. Attitude determines how well you do it."

-- Coach Lou Holtz

"Coaching is a series of conversations, encouragements, and ideas that lead to the creation of your destiny."

-- Honorée Corpron

MASTER STRATEGY #7: UNLOCKING YOUR ALTER EGO WITH A COACH

World-class athletes know it. So do CEOs of major corporations. Winners in nearly every profession know that without the right coach, they won't perform at their peak – with the right coach, the sky is the limit. Now a select number of business people know it, too: as organizations flatten, as production cycles hit hyperspeed, as change becomes a constant, coaches can help you become a better, more nimble, effective and efficient business leader. I absolutely believe everyone needs a coach. Not because I am a coach, but because I have a coach!

Flashing back to my network marketing days – I had achieved a top-level position and was doing everything I needed to do to reach my goals and objectives within the fastest possible time-frame (or so I thought). The CEO of my company called to offer me a business coach and my first thoughts were: "What could I possibly need with a coach?! I'm already doing great!" Fortunately, I kept my mouth shut, accepted the incredible gift of a coach, and I'm so glad I did. Within 90 days I had increased my overall productivity and income by 300%. The distinctions I made about myself, the way I was using my time, identifying bigger goals, defining a larger vision and being held accountable were all crucial to me.

My coach was able to see what I wasn't able to see. She helped me to take risks, eliminate obstacles, and fully step into my potential. I still utilize the services of a coach on an on-going basis.

A coach's function is multi-faceted: to blend insights, tools and key traits to move clients toward success in many areas, both on the job and off. Performers at all levels are elevated to greater advancement in the presence of an effective coach.

As previously mentioned, the value of coaching is clearly understood in the world of sports. Tiger Woods needs a coach to excel. *If the number 1 golfer in the world relies on the power of coaching, wouldn't anyone in the business world benefit from applying the same principle?*

I would venture to guess not a day goes by that Tiger Woods doesn't speak with his "head" coach, or work with his "form" coach to fine-tune his chip shot, drive or putt. Yet many people step into business and leadership positions with little direction, and few goals or strategies for growth and development. Rarely do they seek help acquiring leadership skills or identifying hidden strengths.

Choosing to have a great coach in your corner can accelerate your success. Coaches are not for the meek. They're for people who value unambiguous feedback. The best coaches have one thing in common: they are mercilessly results-oriented. Also, coaching isn't therapy. It's product development, and you are the product.

> *"Coaching is the means through which we come to realize our greatest potential."*
>
> -- Ryan C. Browning
> (my coach)

HOW TO GET THE MOST OUT OF YOUR COACH

INSIST ON COMPLETE CONFIDENTIALITY between the coach and yourself. That means all conversations are private and sacred. It should be part of the coaching agreement you sign. Your coach should not acknowledge you are a client to anyone else unless you give permission. What you are doing, how you are doing, what you have accomplished, and your personal secrets are not discussed or even hinted at with anyone else. People may know you are working with a coach, and may ask how you are doing. Your coach's standard answer should be: "He/she is doing just fine." (Period.)

INSIST ON MEASURABLE GOALS. To ensure that your work with a coach doesn't become an exercise in unproductive conversation, tie everything to a business benefit. By itself, "improve time-management skills" has no measurable benefit. But it's a legitimate way to achieve a critical goal: "meet project deadlines in 30% less time."

SET TANGIBLE GOALS. This isn't the time for stretch goals – aim instead for improvements that you know you can achieve. Most people aren't working on even half their cylinders. Don't strive for 100% improvement -- 15% improvement is the difference between a mediocre player and a star.

When it comes to assessing your performance, ask your coach to be exhaustively honest with you. Some are not. Take these sound bites of coaches describing their role: "I just hold the CEO's hand," says one. "I'm like a trusted family friend," says another. Or: "My job is to remind him, 'your greatest strength is that you're you.'"

If you get that warm, fuzzy feeling from a business coach, run! Look for a coach who isn't afraid to use constructive criticism. Coaches are best when they push you out of your comfort zone -- and don't let you back in.

ARE YOU READY FOR COACHING?

If you're now ready to consider hiring a coach, you are really deciding to embark on a magnificent journey! Coaching is proven to work when two factors are present:

> **The client is willing to grow.**
>
> **There is a gap (or several gaps) between where he/she is now and where he/she wants to be.**

This is all that's necessary for you and your coach to address and resolve challenges, create new focus and direction, move your business in the right direction, dramatically increase sales and profitability, as well as devise and execute a plan of action.

Once you've hired your coach, you will enroll in specific programs that can include:

> **Coaching for skills. The focus on a specific task or skill set, such as making presentations, preparing a business plan, etc.**
>
> **Coaching for performance. Here, the focus is on improving existing job performance and might involve such things as developing systems to accurately evaluate employee performance.**
>
> **Coaching for development, involves concentrating on an individual's future career path.**
>
> **Coaching on a variety of topics. This program recognizes that executives can be lonely and frequently need insight, perspective and constructive feedback on both personal and business issues. It could also include developing specific leadership skills such as emotional intelligence (EQ).**

With some great coaching, you will compress the amount of time it takes to reach your goals. You will also have someone who believes in you, holds your vision for you and can keep you moving in just the right direction. I know you will benefit and enjoy having a coach as much as I do!

ROCKET FUEL

Congratulations! You've completed the book -- a sure sign of your excellence – and your upcoming magnificent success. Clearly you are internally motivated, and it's the internally motivated people in the world who are the most successful.

I have given you some of my most used, tried and true tips, tools, strategies and ideas. I know they work – each and every one of them – because I have used them in the past for great results. I consistently return to them over and over again because I want to create greater future success.

There are no shortcuts. Follow the steps exactly as I've outlined them. Each idea in this book is designed to clear away obstacles and move you more easily toward your goals.

If you've already created your vision, I know you feel you're on fire – invincible even. The goals and the plans you create cement that feeling in your heart – keep you moving in the direction your soul desires. Find and keep in your life those people who desire for you what you desire for yourself. Ask yourself great questions, keep the faith, and don't forget the ultimate secret weapon--your coach.

I did it, and I know you can too. My best wishes for your greatest future success!

"Climb high; Climb far. Your goal the sky; Your aim the star."

--Inscription at Williams College

"Pay your tuition, or get the hell out of here."

-- Graffiti in the men's room at Harvard

DEDICATION

To my precious daughter Alexandra --
everything I do is for you.

HONORÉE

Inspiration • Motivation • Transformation

AUTHOR. Honorée is the author of the book Master Strategies for Explosive Business Growth, and The Referral-Only Business System, a self-study course.

PERSONAL TRANSFORMATION EXPERT. She coaches Fortune 500 CEOs, prominent business owners, entrepreneurs and senior level professionals one-on-one. She specializes in helping individuals achieve their maximum potential. With her strategic coaching, you are guaranteed to dramatically increase your efficiency, effectiveness, achieve your goals and outcomes 60-80% faster than you could do it on your own, all while maintaining integrity, balance and fulfillment.

TURNING SERVICE PROFESSIONALS INTO RAINMAKERS. Honorée gives seminars and conducts training programs on generating business, creating strategic partnerships and practicing exceptional business courtesy for service professionals.

INSPIRING THE MASSES. Honorée presents monthly informational teleseminars, success interviews and online inspirational courses. She presents immediately applicable and practical procedures for focusing vision, goals and actions on the attainment of the life you desire.

THE LEADING EDGE EZINE. Her email magazine reaches thousands of readers each month free of charge.

ACKNOWLEDGEMENTS AND THANKS

To my "inner circle." You know who you are. I remain in awe of you. Thank you for your love and support.

To my clients – I have learned much from you. Thank you.

To Coach Jeff – this book would still be a "to do" on my list without your words of encouragement, accountability and kindness. Thank you.

Honorée Enterprises, Inc.
5836 S. Pecos Road
Las Vegas, Nevada 89120
702.353.5100
www.Corpron.com
Honoree@Corpron.com